MARJORIE PAY HINCKLEY

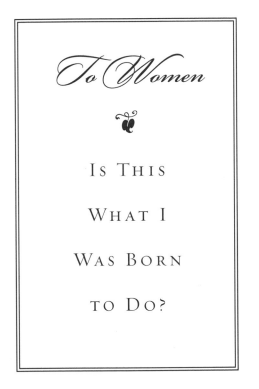

To Women

IS THIS

WHAT I

WAS BORN

TO DO?

DESERET
BOOK

SALT LAKE CITY, UTAH

D0096788

Back cover photo by Don Busath

Visit us at deseretbook.com

ISBN 1-59038-319-2

Printed in the United States of America   71737-093P
Precision Litho, Salt Lake City, UT

10   9   8   7   6   5   4   3   2   1

This is a Cinderella story, but it has far more substance than a simple fairy tale.

Once upon a time, many, many years ago, lived a king who reigned over India and Ethiopia, over a hundred and twenty-seven provinces. In the third year of his reign, he made a feast to show the riches of his glorious kingdom. On the seventh day of the merriment, he sent for his queen, Vashti, to show off her beauty to the people. She refused to come. The king was angry and took from her the royal crown and estate to give to another. The search began for a new queen, and beautiful women were brought from all the provinces.

Now, in one of the provinces lived a Jew whose name was Mordecai. He had raised his uncle's daughter, Esther, since her parents had died. So it came to pass that Mordecai brought Esther to the palace. All the maidens who were brought to be presented to the king were trained and groomed for one year in the women's court at the palace. Finally, it was Esther's turn to be presented to the king. And the king loved Esther above all the women he had seen, and she obtained grace and favor in his sight, and he set the royal crown upon her head and made her his queen.

Now it came to pass that the king's chief adviser hated the Jews and persuaded the king to have all the Jews in his kingdom put to death, and the king agreed to have them all annihilated—men, women, and children—on a certain date.

Mordecai tried to encourage Esther to go to the king and plead for her people. But no one, not even the queen, could enter the presence of the king without being invited. The punishment was death. She would also have to confess that she was a Jew, which the king did not know.

Mordecai tried to encourage her to do what she and only she could do, saying, "Who knoweth whether thou art come to the kingdom for such a time as this?" (Esther 4:14).

Esther asked Mordecai to call upon all the Jews in the land to fast for three days and pray for her. She said, "I also and my maidens will fast likewise; and so will I go in unto the king, which is not according to the law: and if I perish, I perish" (Esther 4:16).

Of course, though I have left out many of the details, you know that Esther's people were saved, and Mordecai was brought into the palace as the king's chief adviser. At this point, the fairy tale would end with, "They all lived happily ever after."

We do not know the end of this story. But we do know that whenever we think of women, we celebrate Esther's very high type of courage, loyalty, and patriotism.

My favorite line of the story is Mordecai's question to her: "Who knoweth whether thou art come to the kingdom for such a time as this?"

Now, let me change the time in history and tell you of an experience I encountered on a Church assignment. This one was in Medford, Oregon, where my husband was assigned to visit a stake conference. We drove from Salt Lake City, arriving at the stake president's home late Saturday afternoon. Some of the children were home. The mother was not. The children told us she was over at the church practicing for an upcoming performance. The twelve-year-old showed us to our bedroom. It was obviously the parents' room. Everything was shiny and clean. The adjoining bathroom had been freshly painted. The paint was barely dry. It was probably finished at midnight on Friday in anticipation of our visit! The fourteen-year-old had just taken a freshly baked blueberry pie from the oven. She had picked the berries that morning and baked the pie herself. On the piano were pictures of the children. They went through them for us. "And who is this one?" I asked, pointing to one on the lamp table of a young man in a white shirt, tie, and dark suit.

"Oh, that's our missionary," she replied with pride. "He's not really our brother, but he came to live with us two years ago, when his parents divorced."

It was soon time for Mother to come home. I knew exactly what she would look like. I had seen her a thousand times in other Mormon homes across the country—a typical, happy, terribly busy mother with the whir of Mormon life going on around her.

I mention these two contrasting experiences to remind you of the very different circumstances that women find themselves in. Perhaps we might take a look at our lives—either in Medford, Oregon, or in the time of King Ahasuerus—and ask ourselves, "Is life fair? Is this what I was born to do?"

Or we might change that question, "Is this what I was born to do?" to another: "Who knoweth whether thou art come to the kingdom for such a time as this?"

President Spencer W. Kimball has said: "Remember, in the world before we came here, faithful women were given certain assignments while faithful men were foreordained to certain priesthood tasks. . . . We are accountable for those things which long ago were expected of us."[1]

Therefore, it would seem important that our greatest quest is to live worthy to know what the Lord's will is regarding us—what we are meant to do.

I love the scripture in the New Testament where the angel appeared to Mary, who was to become the mother of Jesus, and gave her that particular assignment. And she said, "Be it unto me according to thy word" (Luke 1:38).

Some of us are married. Some of us are not (yet). Some of us have children and grandchildren. Some have none.

Some are widowed, some divorced. But we can all do what it is our responsibility to do. We can all bless lives.

I quote from Elaine Cannon: "A woman's significant role is that of being an influence wherever she is. It is her role not only to give life, but to shape life."

Some women are natural leaders. Elaine Cannon was an example to me of leadership. When she served as the Young Women general president she organized a thousand Young Women—all with beautiful banners they had made to express their commitment to the gospel—dressed in white and marched them down the streets of Salt Lake City on the 24th of July to inspire us.

I said, "Thank you." Only an Elaine Cannon could dream up and execute such a spectacle, and we were all cheered and lifted by it. She blessed us all with her leadership. The examples of such inspiring women leaders are all around us.

Some of us are followers, and that is good also, because a leader would have no one to lead without followers. Some of us are what I call "supporters." I concluded long ago that my happiest role was that of a supporter. To me personally, this is a great and extremely satisfying role.

During World War II, we were encouraged to plant gardens, not only by the Church but by the government. My husband dug three thousand holes in the property to the south of our home and planted three thousand tomato plants. He hoed them and weeded them and irrigated them at 4:30 every Monday morning. When the tomatoes were ripe, I spent my days picking them. Baskets full, boxes full. We put up a sign: "Tomatoes for Sale." Toward the end of the crop, we couldn't give them away. My back ached.

I could have said, "Is this what I was born to do?"

But the tomatoes went on people's food shelves, and the money we were paid for them paid the taxes that year, the taxes on our house, the house that gave us shelter and was a home for our children. The whole project gave my husband and me a sense of "togetherness." The wife does not walk in front of or behind her husband, but at his side. And what is a blessing for him is a blessing for her. I have never felt to apologize to anyone for my supporting role as a wife and mother.

Let me tell you about a beautiful girl, who during the first year of her married life lived in New York City. She had graduated from BYU in fashion design and was blessed to find an exciting job in the corporate headquarters of J. C. Penney, near Rockefeller Center. Her very responsible job was to choose what clothes would go into a large section of their catalog, which went to catalog subscribers all across the nation. It was exciting. She loved it.

Then came the impending arrival of her first baby. One day, a few months before the baby was born, she told her boss that she would soon resign. Her co-workers couldn't believe it. Why would she give up a promising career in New York to become "just a housewife"?

"I'm not leaving to become a housewife," she said. "I'm

leaving to become a homemaker, the most wonderful career of all."

JoAnn Ottley, wife of the conductor of the Mormon Tabernacle Choir and an accomplished soprano, has blessed our lives with her beautiful music. She has successfully combined a partial career with homemaking. I heard her husband say that when she had finished her studies in Europe and the opportunities were there for her to become a professional opera star, she said to her husband, "I would rather go home and sing to my Relief Society sisters."

She did just that, but as the years have passed she has had more than enough opportunities to improve upon her talents and yet rear her family, too.

I once heard the story of a lawyer, the daughter of Supreme Court Justice Powell, who left her law profession to stay home with her firstborn. She said, "Anyone can take care of my clients. Only I can be the mother of this child." Her decision was easily made—not in terms of rights, but in terms of responsibility and love.

I would like to share with you the beautiful words of Neal Maxwell on this subject. "When the real history of mankind is fully disclosed, will it feature the echoes of gunfire or the shaping sound of lullabies? The great armistices made by military men or the peacemaking of women in homes and neighborhoods? Will what happened in the cradles and kitchens prove to be more controlling than what happened in congresses? When the surf of centuries has made the great pyramids so much sand, the everlasting family will still be standing, because it is a celestial institution."[2]

Having said all this for the benefit of those who feel they are only housewives and mothers, I also want to pay tribute to the women who for a variety of reasons are combining child rearing with careers outside of the home. It isn't easy for you. You are working very hard, long hours, for you understand, also, the importance of home and child rearing. And you are in many instances unbelievably successful in both areas.

Each of us—married, single, widowed, divorced, housewives, career women, students, grandmothers—can ask ourselves each morning, "What can I do to make life happier for someone today?" Sometimes all it takes is just a few kind words to a clerk in the grocery store. Sometimes it is steady service over a lifetime.

Let me tell you about my grandfather's sister, who was an important person in my childhood. Aunt Nellie was a nurse. She never married. But when Mother's babies were born, Aunt Nellie would come up from her home in American Fork and move in with us for a week or so and take care of Mother and the new baby. She has been gone now for over fifty years, but when my ninety-one-year-old mother was floating in and out of consciousness during her last illness, she kept saying, "Oh, if only Nellie were here. She could make me comfortable."

We all have our place, our important something we can

do in our own individual way—something no one else can do for us—our own unique opportunity to serve.

And let us approach our duties with an attitude of excellence. As Anne Osborn Poelman wrote: "One only has to look at a sunset, or a starry night, to know that God did everything in excellence, not in a cheap or easy way."

I read in the paper of a woman who had made an excellent career as a cleaning woman. She had gone to work after the death of her husband. She was untrained, and the most immediate work she could find was to become a cleaning woman. She became so proficient and innovative in finding the very best and most efficient and inexpensive ways to perform all the household cleaning jobs that she ended up writing and publishing a book on the subject.

The gospel calls to us to stretch ourselves, to embrace our talents, to concentrate on our strengths, to be productive, to be creative, to reach our full potential, which few of us ever do. In the words of Robert Louis Stevenson: "To be what we are, and to become what we are capable of becoming, is the only end of life."[3]

Let us not waste our time saying with bitterness, "Is this what I was born to do?" Let us rather ask ourselves the question that was asked of Esther: "Who knoweth whether thou art come to the kingdom for such a time as this?"

Perhaps what you are doing, whatever it is or however humble your offering, could be something that no one else could do in quite the same way. Say to yourself: "The world is my oyster. I am in control. There is no limit to what I can do."

Be thankful and be glad!

I truly believe that if we keep the commandments as we understand them and accept our responsibilities with gladness, the day will come in the eternities when God will say to us, male and female: "Well done, thou good and faithful servant: thou hast been faithful over a few things, I will make thee ruler over many things" (Matthew 25:21).

God bless us all to this end.

NOTES

1. *My Beloved Sisters* (Salt Lake City: Deseret Book, 1979), 37.

2. "The Women of God," *Ensign*, May 1978, 10–11.

3. Stevenson, *Familiar Studies of Men and Books* (London: Chatto and Windus, 1882).